# FUNERAL ORATION FOR BESSARION

Michael Apostolius

Translated by: D.P. Curtin

Dalcassian Publishing Company
PHILADELPHIA, PA

Copyright @ 2007 Dalcassian Publishing Company

All rights reserved. No part of this publication may be reproduced, distributed, or transmitted in any form or by any means, including photocopying, recording, or other electronic or mechanical methods, without the prior written permission of the publisher, except in the case of brief quotations embodied in critical reviews and certain other non-commercial uses permitted by copyright law. For permission request, write to Dalcassian Publishing Company at dalcassianpublishing at gmail.com

ISBN: 979-8-8691-6803-0 (Paperback)

Library of Congress Control Number:
Author: Curtin, D.P. (1985-)

Printed by Ingram Content Group, 1 Ingram Blvd, La Vergne, Tennessee

First printing edition 2007.

# FUNERAL ORATION FOR BESSARION

A FUNERAL ORATION'S PREAMBLE

# TO THE MOST REVEREND BESSARION, CARDINAL OF SAINT SABINA AND THE HOLY PATRIARCH OF CONSTANTINOPLE.

Therefore, it was in my fate that, after those many calamities and the conquest and destruction of the sacred and dearest peerage to me, I should scarcely be revived, and should hear this intolerable news. Our wisest and most divine master and supporter, whom nations and states, churches and principalities wished to have as a counselor and governor in all things, of men, alas! It was taken unexpectedly! Oh, the misfortunes of a long time, and the sudden reversals of things, and the ebbs and flows of fortune, what have you accomplished in our age, digesting this long ago, when either before or after our times it was permissible? Shall I not say, as was the case, that the supreme controller of things took vengeance on us for the calamities which preceded it? Or did he supersede this as if it were due! Would that he would deliver!

Therefore, if I had decided that I would now incur so many evils and inflict these most fatal punishments, I would have preferred to be burned at that time, slaughtered by the (Persians) Achaemenids, then to suffer the calamities of six hundred worse deaths in the miserable fallen fortune. For, as Euripides says, "it is better to die once than to suffer evil all the days".

O, you who see with your most perceptive eye what is happening! O most wise of those who are under the sun and above the sun, manager, why did you extinguish the most splendid torch of the world? Or rather, why did you pluck out that sun-shining eye? Was he not a worshiper of piety? Is not the defender of the Church? Don't I hate evil? Are you not a lover of justice? Isn't it wise? Did he not decorate the whole world with his virtues? Was not the needy daily fed? Was he not bloodless, as many days went by, as he made sacrifices incessantly? Isn't everything that can be said to be both good and just and religious? O wisdom, virtue, and discipline, which of you destroys a residence so well-polished, that it would not be otherwise? For not only the Greeks and Romans, and all who love their yoke and are ruled by them, admire the wisdom and all the rest of this man's beauty, but also Britons and Cimbri and Germans, Celts and Gauls and Spaniards, Paeons and Iberians and Celtiberians. I will say, the entire Greek and barbarian race, among whom it is attaining a glory that reaches even to heaven, and from there, as I think, will have a memory that will abundantly surpass the nature of all time.

Alas! Who has cast away my hope of good things reduced to ashes? Who took away my children's food? Who has snatched away the comforter of my old age and the companionship of old poverty? The affairs of the country and the state are nothing to me, nor the loss of children, nor the bereavement of fathers, nor the throwing away of houses and money, nor any other of these things which bring pain and sickness, and the like, by falling upon poor men. Most gracious Bessarion, I must certainly honor and sweet honor and property and name, such as you were to us and then, hey to me! You are dead! You persisted in dealing with me not as a master, not as a benefactor or the wisest, but as if you were equal in fortune and indebted to me, or even as if you knew some philosophy of manners and dogmas.

Would that the bones and the nerves and the flesh and the muscles and the fat and the cartilages with the marrow and all the coagulation of the fluids in me, having been divinely transformed into fountains of tears, would flow to me as I say these things! For otherwise I could not sufficiently praise that prince of letters and of wisdom himself, more eloquent than Plato, more vehement than Demosthenes, with the majesty and beauty of his elegant orations, the one who shed darkness with the sublimity of Thucydides, who by the insoluble conclusions of syllogisms showed himself to be by no means surpassed by Aristotle and Chrysippus, and of all the Cardinals himself, or of his Father's father, whether he likes it or not, he was honorable and a crown.

Now Orpheus, and the Muses, and Homer, now Gorgias, and Lysias, and Andocides, now Pherecydes, Pythagoras, and Plato, should have been present, that they might write hymns, funeral orations, and epigrams upon a man of virtues, a model and image, if even those hymns could equal his praise. As for me, when I am one, when I am a little man, and yet I dare to join a preacher and to sing a monody and to continue with a funeral oration at last, who would not be rightly enraged? Are not reproaches hurled at us, who attempt those things which we cannot reach, and which are beyond our strength? But none of these matters to me, provided you speak as though you were alive, and so certainly and after death you will gladly accept them.

Moreover, it was his country which, after the queen city of the cities, was the most ancient queen of Trapezus, and the Greek city sung by the philosophers in six hundred places of writing, and whoever among them had the heart to organize a city that was prosperous, well established by laws, having letters, rightly arranged in all things, for form and they proposed Trapeze as a model.

But the parents were not of the nobles and distinguished by fortune, but they made a living by hand and artifice, a living, as I truly believe, a more just and divine life than that of tyrants and dynasts, who rule and rule nations and states; and those to whom they themselves are subject to fortune and chance, they make slaves of their children by force, and compel them to pay tributes and taxes and exactions, and those who neither give nor have wherewith to give are threatened with extremity, and Pluto himself, who is blind and is said to be blind, is brought forth with rage against them. But these, though they have none of all these things, still live kindly and according to nature, more abundantly than the rich, bringing help to the needy from their labors, receiving strangers as hospitality, and with a more zealous spirit, they kindle the fire, anoint with oil, clothe them, and make them lie down.

But after he had grown up to boyhood, Dositheus, the great antistitutus of Trapezuntius, took him with him, having been sealed by his parents, whom he trained with many prayers, supplications, and words, and at the same time adopted him as his own son, and indeed far more glorious than he who was born according to nature. But when it came to his mind to restore Byzantium, he brought with him a boy bearing before him the beauty of virtue, and not long after the teacher, whose life was blameless and incorruptible, by experience he cast into the hands of a most expert, knowing very well that the rest of what is good in men is of little firmness and of a very short time, but that discipline in us is immortal and which cannot be taken away.

Moreover, having attained that which he held with great desire, he made that first art necessary to all the others that follow it, more quickly by the hope of all, by study, by the acumen of the mind, and by a good character; He also established the multiple parts of poetry, so that it should be a rich and copious art, able to express all the feelings of the soul with the equipment of language and the multitude of names, and to express with complete clarity and with the greatest ease the kind of operation, or attitude, or affection, or greatness that men or even gods have been allotted to each one. Then in rhetoric, which breathes with the power of fire, although he himself stayed with the comisel, he far surpassed the others either in deliberating, or in stating the reasons, or in the kind of demonstration. But when he had mastered this very well and by desire, he had a desire to learn logic and ethics, and those things which are of nature and ideas, and he succeeded in the matter well, although he had not studied very much at all, nor for a long time. But of the arts and sciences of mathematics, in a short time indeed, having (Gesthimus) Plethon as his guide, he perceived the best of all. But the rest, as if superfluous to those who worshiped piety and useless, he left to those who wished to inquire into it. Therefore, with a man thus behaving in these matters, and having divided his twofold cares, on the one hand in literature, without which life is blind, and on the other in the training of the institution by which one lives worthy of God, the time came at last, much desired by both peoples, when he united the broken nations and that ancient he dissolves enmity, peace and harmony, he brings back all the most beautiful and useful things in life.

Alas! Who can handle and tell them without tears? For what reason are my pitiful eyes dried up, and all my limbs seized with horror, except because the blood from the pain around my heart has hardened my external parts without reason? At that time, therefore, they begged and forced our noble citizen, who had advanced to manhood, to become the most famous archbishop of Nicaea. From there, together with our most serene emperor and with him who at that time governed the reins of the Church, and with all the senate of the Eastern Church, he set sail for Italy. But those who had assembled there wanted the best of both peoples to be chosen as patrons of their respective causes, and they chose this one of them first. And how much he said, and how much he wrote in that sacred and most divine synod, and in that which was held in another part of Italy, they felt, and those who were there at that time, felt, and those who were concerned with what happened afterwards, will feel, indeed, even those who will , when it is permissible to read the most numerous and excellent speeches of the man by hand.

Oh, how many then admired you! how many have congratulated our nation on account of you! How many children preached and praised the blessed father! How many are blessed by the most divine Dositheus, because of your institution! Furthermore, because of these things and twice more, the Romans decorated you with the dignity of a cardinal, and in addition you became their patriarch, which was not so long ago, Lei me! They established that she was the queen of the states. Nay, indeed, thou art judged worthy to be raised to the highest and most divine pinnacle of the Roman pontificate and would indeed have been raised had it not been for the hindrance of the unhappiness of our nation, or rather the all-seeing eye of God placing another in the future which human knowledge cannot grasp.

Now, when he was such and such a great man, compelled by nature to concede, God transferred him from this mortal and corruptible life into an incorruptible and immortal one; indeed, we were not worthy to enjoy so much beauty for a long time.

It is not hidden from me, my dearest friends, that men and most people think of no pain more acute than that which leads to death; As for me, I consider that there is no sweeter pleasure than to leave this life. for when they are, as it were, held in prison custody, with fetters and punishments, they are brought forth by them to an immortal and most delightful life, and God appoints them guardians to himself, rewarding some with a higher seat, and others with a lower seat, according to the measure of each one's struggles, rewarding him with dignity.

Verily, perverted men, overwhelmed by ancient pleasures, as if intoxicated with a heavier drink throughout their whole life, consider this prison for an inexorable meadow, and do not wish to loose their bonds, seeing that they prefer these lowest things to the highest. But for me it is neither of these nor of such. But those who have preferred the heavenly to the earthly, unless it were to the greatest detriment even in that part of themselves which is more important, would have exposed themselves to error six hundred times, and would have lost their most divine life and seat. Now no one would have inquired into this from the beginning, unless he thought that what is in us is the most important thing to be immortal.

Moreover, that the better and more divine part of us remains immortal, and it has been demonstrated by many others by long reasonings, and by these of ours, though brief and needy, I think that it will not be obvious. First of all, because it is the most ancient, this dogma is the most celebrated in the mouth of many, not only among the vulgar and lowly, whether older or more recent races of men, but also among those nations which are the most numerous and praised under the sun. If this were not the most persuasive, they would not think that those who had lived a just and holy life, after their death in the fields of Elysium, would dwell in all kinds of happiness, safe from pain and all evils, nor would they pay homage to the dead, nor do anything else that they were supposed to give to the dead.

Then, unless things were so, no one would think anything divine, nor understand the cause, and therefore would not be affected by the desire for infinity or eternity. And this is evident to all who have ever been born and perished among men of all ages. Therefore, the soul is immortal and eternal.

Moreover, do not see any of those things that kill oneself. Moreover, there are men who lay hands on themselves and seek death. It is clear that the soul is immortal; otherwise, man would never willingly rush into his own destruction. But now he does this, knowing that what is most important in himself, nay, that which is himself, not only to remain and continue, but to cross over to better seats than those here, with a broken bond.

Moreover, everything that is not dissolved by its own vice is incorruptible; but the soul is not dissolved by its own vice; moreover, the vice of the soul is timidity, envy, lasciviousness, and all the rest of this kind. Therefore, the soul is incorruptible and immortal.

But still everything that moves itself is always moved; But what is always moving is restless; further, the restless end that before the end you have seen, immortal. Moreover, such is the soul. It is clear, then, that he is mortal and that the end is experienced also from this, that many of those who are in it are to depart from this life, at the very exit, they foretell the definite deaths of many, not only of those who are in the same city, but also of those who are far off who are serving in fate. I certainly saw it with my own eyes and heard that it happened from the mouth of others. It is true that they would neither foretell nor foretell the death of others except through the foresight of the soul, which is immortal and always inquires through it, and what it provides, and what it does, and what it desires and from whom it abstains.

And indeed, O friends, let this be enough for us at the present time, since we cannot better thank our most divine husband and leader for want of words and humility, and we know that others composed far more beautiful funeral orations and epigrams than ours; benefits But you, having looked at the other virtues of the man, and remembering that he was the model of true and divine wisdom, must be considered blessed and most fortunate. He promised his new disciples that he would drink with the faithful in that first and most beautiful and just kingdom of his, which I already promise to those who are worthy, that is, from those that God has signified to us who foresees the future.

# LATIN TEXT

## ORATIO FUNEBRIS LAMENTABILE HABENS PROOEMIUM IN DIVINISSIMUM BESSARIONEM REVERENDISSIMUM CARDINALEM SANCTÆ SABINÆ ET SANCTISSIMUM PATRIARCHAM CONSTANTINOPOLITANUM.

Ergo erat in fatis ut, post plurimas illas calamitates et sacræ mihique charissimæ pairiæ expugnationem et excidium, vixdum recreatus, et hunc intolerabilem nuntium audirem. Sapientissimum nostrum et divinissimum dominum et fautorem, quem gentes et civitates, ecclesiæque et principatus consiliarium et præsidem in omnibus habere exoptabant, ex hominibus, heu! Inopinato fuisse sublatum! O longi temporis infortunia et subitæ rerum conversiones refluæque fortunæ, quid hoc jamdudum concoquentes nostra ætate perfecistis, cum vel ante vel nostra post tempora liceret? Annon diguam, ut par fuit, ultionem a nobis sumpsit summus rerum moderator per eas quæ praecesserunt calamitates? an et ultimam hanc quasi debitam superinduxit; ut cum ipsa et vitain nobis, heu! Utinam eriperet!

Ideo, hoc quidem si presidissem me tanta in mala nunc incursurum et has funestissimas daturum poenas, libentius optassem tunc temporis comburi, Achæmenidarum acinace interemptum, quam in miseram delapsum fortunam sexcentis pejores mortibus subire calamitates. Satius est enim, ut ait Euripides, semel mori quam cunctis diebus male perpeti.

O tu qui perspicacissimo ea quæ fiunt oculo conspicis! O sapientissime eorum, quæ sub sole sunt et super solem, dispensator, ad quid splendidissimam orbis facem exstinxisti? Vel potius quare illum sole fulgentiorem oculum eruisti? Nonne pietatis cultor erat? Nonne Ecclesiæ defensor? Nonne malorum osor? Nonne justitiæ amans? Nonne sapientissimus? Nonne suis virtutibus orbem universum decorabat? Nonne egenis quotidie opitulabatur? Nonne incruenta, quotquot eunt dies, sacrificia indesinenter faciebat? Nonne quidquid dici potest et boni, et justi, et religiosi? O sapientia, virtusque et disciplina, quis vestrum dissolvit domicilium ita optime perpolitum, ut aliter non liceret? Hujus enim viri sapientiam et omnem reliquum decorem non modo Græci et Romani et quicunque eorum jugum amant ab iisque reguntur in admirgtione habent, sed et Britanni et Cimbri et Germani, Celtæque et Galli atque Hispani, Pæonesque et Iberes ac Celtiberes, atque, ut uno verbo dicam, Græcanicum genus omne et barbaricum, apud quos gloriam adeptns est quæ cœlum usque pertingat et memoriam exinde, ut reor, habebit quæ omnis temporis naturam abunde sit superatura.

Eheu! quis mihi bonorum spem in cineres redactam confudit? Quis mihi puerorum nutritium abstulit? quis mihi senilis ætatis et consociæ senio paupertatis rapuit consolatorem? Nihil mihi ad hoc reputatæ sunt res patriæ civitatis, nihil liberorum amissio, nihil patrum orbitas, nihil domorum et pecuniarum jactara , neque quidquam aliud horum quæcunque dolorem et morbum et his affinia miseris hominibus ingruendo afferunt. Osapientissime Bessarion, venerandum certe mihi et dulce decus et res et nomen, qualis fuisti nobis et deinde, hei mihi! Mortuus es! Qui mecum non quasi dominus conversari perseverasti, non quasi benefactor aut sapientissimus, sed quasi qui fortuna æqualis et mihi debitor esses, vel etiam quasi cum sciente nonnihil philosophiæ morum et dogmatum.

Utinam mihi hæc dicenti nunc ossa et nervi atque caro musculique et adipes et cum medulla cartilagines et omnis in me succorum concretio divinitus transmutata in lacrymarum fontes diffluerent! Aliter enim non satis digne deflere possim litterarum ipsiusque sapientiæ principem illum, Platone disertiorem, vehementiorem Demosthene, sua in concinnandis orationibus majestate et pulchritudine, Thucydidæ sublimitati tenebras offundentem, illum qui insolubilibus syllogismorum conclusionibus nequaquam se ab Aristotele et Chrysippo superatum esse demonstravit, omniumque cardinalium ipsiusque Patris patrum velint nolint, decus et corona fuit.

Nunc adesse oporteret Orphea, Museumque et Homerum, nunc Gorgiam et Lysiam et Andociden, nunc Pherecyden, Pythagoramque et Platonem, ut in virum virtutum exemplar et imaginem hymnos et funebres orationes et epigrammata conscriberent, si tamen et illi hymnis eum celebrare pares esse possent. Mihi vero, cum sim unus, cum sim lantillus, et tamen præconium contexere audeam et monodiam decantare funebrique oratione denique prosequi, quis non jure succenseat? Quæve in nos non jactentur convicia, qui ea quæ attingere non possumus et supra vires sunt attentamus? Sed nihil horum mihi curæ est, dummodo tu sermones, ut vivens, ita certe et post mortem libenter accipias.

Porro illi erat patria quæ post reginam urbem urbium fuit regina Trapezus antiquissima et Græca civitas a philosophis in sexcentis scriptorum locis decantata et quibuscunque inter ipsos cordi fuit prospere se habentem ordinare civitatem, legibus bene constitutam, forentem litteris, recte in omnibus dispositam, ii pro forma et exemplari Trapezuntem proposuerunt.

Parentes autem non ex nobilibus erant et fortuna insignibus, sed manu et artificio victum transigebant, victum, ut ego quidem reor, justiorem divinioremque tyrannorum victu dynastarumque, qui gentes et civitates imperio tenent et dirigunt: illi namque homines iisdem affectionibus inditos ex iisdem procreatos sanguinibus, et iisdem quibus ipsi fortunis et casibus obnoxios, ex liberis servos vi faciunt, atque tributa vectigaliaque et exactiones solvere cogunt, et non præbentibus neque habentibus unde præbeant extrema minitantur, et Pluto ipso qui cæcus est ac dicitur cæciores in eos rabie efferantur. Hi autem, etsi nihil horum omnium habentes sint, boneste tamen et secundum naturam vivunt, copiosius quam divites propriis ex laboribus egenis opem ferentes, peregrinos hospitio suscipientes, alacriorique animo ignem accendunt, ungunt oleo, vestimentis induunt et accumbere faciunt.

Postquam vero in pueritiam provectus est, optimna nota signatum eum a parentibus secum assumpsit maximus antistitum Trapezuntius Dositheus, quem multis omnino precibus obsecrationibusque et verbis institueret, simulque in filium sibi adoptaret et quidem longe gloriosiorem eo qui secundum naturam genitus. Cum autem ipsi in mentem venisset Byzantium remeare, secum adduxit et puerum virtutis pulchritudinem præ se ferentem, nec multo post magistro, cujus vita irreprehensa, incorruptique mores, ob experientiam peritissimo in manus iradidit, apprime sciens cætera quæ sunt in hominibus bona parum esse firma et brevissimi temporis, disciplinam vero in nobis immortalem esse et quæ auferri nequeat.

Porro id cujus magno tenebatur desiderio assecutus, omnium spe citius, studio, mentis accumine et bona indole primam artem illam, cæteris omnibus quæ eam sequuntur necessariam condidicit; condidicit et multiplices poeticæ partes, ut quæ sit ars locuples et copiosa, linguæ apparatu et nominum multitudine omnes animi sensus exprimere valens, et qualem vel operationem, vel habitum, vel affectionem, vel magnitudinem sortitus sit hominum aut etiam deorum unusquisque dilucide omnino et facillime commonstrans. Tunc in rhetorica, quæ vim ignis spirat, etsi comis ipse el moratus, cæteros sive in deliberando, sive in causis dicendis, sive in demonstrandi genere longe superabat. Cum autem hæc optime et ex voto calluit, logicam porro et ethicam et eas quæ sunt de natura et ideis sciendias discere in desiderio habuit, eique res bene successit, quin tamen multum prorsus nec diu studuisset. Mathematicarum vero artium et scietiarum, brevi quidem tempore, Plethonem habens ducem, optima quæque percepit. Sed reliqua, quasi supervacua pietatem colentibus et inutilia, iis qui vellent inquirenda dimisit. Ergo iis de rebus ita se habente viro et bifariam curas partito, hinc quidem in litteras, sine quibus cæca est vita, illinc vero in exercitationem instituti quo Deo digne vivitur, venit tandem tempus illud, utrisque populis desideratissimum, quod disruptas gentes coadunavit et antiquam illam dissolvit inimicitiam, pacemque et concordiam, res omnium quæ sunt in vita pulcherrimas et utilissimas reduxit.

Heu! qui sine lacrymis illa tracto et enarro? Quam ob causam miserrimi oculi mei sunt exsiccati, et omnia membra mea horrore coercita, nisi quia sanguis præ dolore circum præcordia concretus exteriora mea non absque ratione induravit? Eo igitur tempore virilem in aetatem progressum nobilem nostrum civem, ut celeberrimæ Nicæ chiepiscopus fieret et rogaverunt et coegerunt. Exinde, una cum serenissimo imperatore nostro et cum eo qui tunc temporis Ecclesiæ habenas regebat, cumque omni Orientalis Ecclesiæ senatu, in Italiam vela fecit. Qui vero illuc convenerant, voluerunt utrique ex utrisque populis optimos quosque suæ ipsorum causæ patronos deligi, et hunc unum ex illis in primis elegerunt. Quam multa autem dixerit, quamque multa conscripserit in sacra illa divinissimaque synodo et in ea quæ alia in parte Italiæ est habita, senserunt et ii quicunque tunc illic ade rant, senserunt et ii quibus curæ fuerunt ea quæ postmodum gesta sunt, sentient vero etiamnum qui volent, cum liceat plurimas et optimas viri orationes manu usurpatas perlegere.

O quam multi tunc in admiratione te habuerunt! quam multi propter te genti nostræ gratulati sunt! Quam multi prole felicissimum patrem beatum prædicaverunt et laudaverunt! Quam multi divinissimo Dositheo, tuæ institutionis causa, faustissima sunt appreciati! Porro propter hæc et bis adhuc plura, te Romani cardinalis dignitate decorarunt, et insuper te patriarcham ejus quæ non ita multo anten, Lei mihi! civitatum regina fuit constituerunt. Quin imo dignus es judicatus qui ad summum et divinissimum Romani pontificatus apicem evehereris, et quidem evectus esses nisi fuisset impedimento nostræ gentis infelicitas, vel potius Dei omnia pervidentis oculus alia in futurum reponens quæ hominuo scientia capere non potest.

Illum vero, cum talis ac tantus esset, naturæ concedere coactum, ex hac mortali et corruptibili vita in incorruptain et immortalem transtulit Deus; quippe haud digni fuimus qui diu tanto decore frueremur.

Non me quidem latet, amicissimi viri, homines plerosque nullum existimare dolorem acriorem eo qui ad mortem ducit; ego vero Donis nullam esse suaviorem censeo voluptatem quam ex hac vita migrationem; quia, cum sint quasi in carceralibus custodiis, compedibusque et suppliciis detenti, ab iis educti ad immortalem jucundissimamque vitam transmigrant, et eos Deus paredros sibi constituit, sedis alios quidem altioris, alios autem inferioris, juxta uniuscujusque certaminum mensuram, dignitate remunerans.

Verum perversi homines, voluptatis veterno obruti, quasi graviore potu per totam vitam inebriati, pro immarcescibili prato hunc carcerem habent neque vincula dissolvi cupiunt, quippe qui infima hæc supernis præponant. Mihi autem neque de his neque de talibus est sermo. Sed qui præ terrenis coelestia præelegerunt, nisi id etiam in ea sui parte quæ potior est maximo esset detrimento, sexcenties sese errore exuissent, divinissimam vitam et sedem sor tituri. Hoc autem a principio nullus inquisivisset, nisi esse immortale id quod in nobis est præcipuum existimaret.

Porro meliorem divinioremque nostri partem immortalem permanere, et a multis aliis per longas ratiocinationes demonstratum est, et per hasce nostras, breves licet et egenas baud inevidens fore arbitror. Primum quidem, quia antiquissimum est, hoc dogma et multorum ore celebratissimum , non solum apud vulgaria et ignobilia, sive vetustiora , sive recentiora hominum genera, sed et apud eas gentes quæ sub sole sunt plurimas et laudatissimas. Quibus nisi id esset persuasissimum, neque eos qui juste et sancte vixerunt, post obitum in Elysios campos abeuntes, in omnimoda felicitate doloris malorumque omnium securos habitare opinarentur, neque defunctis adhiberent obsequia, nec quidquam aliud eorum quæ mortuis conferre arbiIrarentur.

Deinde, nisi ita se res haberet , nullus quidquam divini existimaret, neque causam intelligeret, ideoque nec infinitatis nec æternitatis desiderio afficeretur.

Hoc autem evidens omnibus qui unquam ex omni ævo nati sunt et interierunt hominibus. Immortalis ergo et sempiterna est anima.

Præterea nullum videas eorum quæ sunt seipsum ultro interimere. Porro ex hominibus sunt qui sibi ipsi manus inferunt et mortem oppetunt. Patet immortalem esse animam; sin minus , homo nunquam proprium in interitum libens irrueret. Nunc autem hoc facit, sciens id quod in se præcipuum est, imo id quod est ipse, non solum constare et permanere, sed ad meliores quam quæ hic sunt sedes, abrupto vinculo, jam transmeare.

Insuper id omne quod per proprium vitium non dissolvitur incorruptibile est; atqui anima per proprium vitium non dissolvitur porro vitium est animæ timiditas, invidia, lascivia et cætera quælibet bujusmodi; incorruptibilis ergo anima et immortalis.

Adhuc autem omne quod seipsum movet semper movetur; quod vero semper movetur irrequietum est; porro irrequietum finis exper; quod antem finis expers, immortale. Porro talis est anima. Iumortalem igitur et finis expertem esse etiam ex hoc patet, quod multi eorum qui in eo sunt ut ex hac vita decedant, ipso in exitu, definitas multorum mortes prædicunt non eorum tantummodo qui eadem in urbe sed et qui procul fato funguntur. Ego certe id ipsissimis oculis vidi et ex aliorum ore hæc evenisse audivi. Verum mortem aliorum neque prænoscerent neque prædicerent nisi per prævisionem animæ quæ immortalis est idque semper inquirit per ea et quæ providet, et quæ agit, et quæ cupit et quibus abstinet.

Et hæc quidem, O amici , in præsenti satis sint nobis, quippe qui sermonum inopia et humilitate divinissimo viro ducique nostro melius gratias referre non possimus, et alios noverimus longe pulchriores nostra funebres orationes et epigrammata composuisse, quoscunque circumiens honorabat, omnigenisque optimis et magnificentissimis cumulabat beneficiis. Vos autem, inspectis cæteris viri virtutibus, memoresque ipsum veræ divinæque sapientiæ exemplar exstitisse, beatum felicissimumque arbitrari oportet: Deum vero omnia pervidentem eos homines qui præclare et sancte vixerunt, inter quos unus erat et hic noster fautor bonus, religiosus, liberalis, temperans, intelligenes, magnanimus, et hoc certe ipsum sciens quis sit vir sensu præditus beatusque, hos, inquam, qui tales sunt semper propriam in domum ad se evocare, et quem ob virtutes dilexerit eum illic commorari jubere et convivam factum vinum bibere nectare et ambrosia suavius, quod novum cum fidelibus se bibiturum discipulis suis pollicitus est in primo illo suo et pulcherrimo et justissimo regno, quod jamjam his qui digni sunt spondeo, ex iis nempe quæ nobis significavit qui futura prævidet Deus.

The Scriptorium Project is the work of a small group of lay people of various apostolic churches who are interested in the preservation, transmission, and translation of the works of the early and medieval church. Our efforts are to make the works of the church fathers accessible to anyone who might have an interest in Christian antiquities and the theological, philosophical, and moral writings that have become the bedrock of Western Civilization.

To-date, our releases have pulled from the Greek, Syriac, Georgian, Latin, Celtic, Ethiopian, and Coptic traditions of Christianity, and have been pulled from sundry local traditions and languages.

# Other Selections from the Byzantine Church Series:

*Funeral Oration for Bessarion* by Michael Apostolius (Mar. 2007)
*Treatise on Sobriety* by Nicephorus the Solitary (Apr. 2007)
*Sermons* by Nestorius of Constantinople (May 2009)
*Theophrastus* by Aeneas of Gaza (Apr. 2011)
*Treatise on Prayer* by St. Evargius of Ponticus (May 2011)
*The Lausiac History* by St. Palladius of Galatia (Mar. 2013)
*Letter on the Fall of Constantinople* by Isidore of Kiev (Oct. 2013)
*The Hesychast* by Gregory of Sinai (June 2015)
*Selected Laws* by Justinian I, Emperor of Rome (July 2018)
*Exhortation to Monks Ordained in India* by St. John of Karpathos (March 2021)
*Fragments of 'Chronicle'* by Hippolytus of Thebes (May 2023)
*The Life of the Blessed Theotokos* by Epiphanius Monachus (July 2023)
*Letters of Nestorius* by Nestorius of Constantinople (Sept. 2023)

www.ingramcontent.com/pod-product-compliance
Lightning Source LLC
LaVergne TN
LVHW061044070526
838201LV00073B/5168